Snapshots From A Country Diary

Sprinkled with Humor

Kathryn,

Faye A. Little, R.N.

*Thank you for your love
and support all through
these years!*

Faye Aderek Little
March 9, 2019

ISBN: 9781794383715

DEDICATION

This book is dedicated to the many people who made a living from the land, having the faith that they would survive all circumstances. One person who practiced that belief in his daily life was my Daddy, Thomas Adcock. He had the gift of sharing with others his wisdom and knowledge of the very basic skills needed for tough circumstances. Although he never had the opportunity for a school education beyond the fifth grade, his wisdom and good common sense prevailed beyond his years. Many people in the small community of Berea, North Carolina, sought his advice on cows, hogs, chickens, and growing tobacco. Today, he might be called a "Consultant Farmer." To all the people who knew him and are reading this book, I hope you enjoy his shadow in my stories. Many of you can probably recall something he told you that made you laugh. I carry that trait with me at all times. To God be the glory, great things He and Daddy hath done.

Proverbs 17:22 "A merry heart doeth good like a medicine: but a broken spirit drieth the bones.

Faye A. Little, R.N.

Much of Faye Little's nursing career involved persons dealing with substance abuse issues.

She wishes to extend her support to Cross Roads Reconciliation Services in Danville, Virginia , a faith- based community service organization, offering hope to women in recovery. A portion of the proceeds from her book will be donated to this ministry.

For more information, visit the Website: crossroadstruthhouse.org

Snapshots From A Country Diary

Sprinkled With Humor

CONTENTS

Snapshots From A Country Diary

Sprinkled With Humor

ACKNOWLEDGMENTS

I wish to thank all of the people who left footprints in my heart and memories to share. Most of the stories are about life on the farm and the dynamics of a large family living in the country. I extend much appreciation to former teachers, preachers, and the congregation of all the churches I have attended over the years. I am grateful for the friendships made during my thirty -year work experience in a State Mental Hospital in Butner, North Carolina. The patients and coworkers taught me to accept people as they are and to give encouragement to those who did not like themselves. I've learned to focus on the wellness part of people. We are all patients in transition on a continuum from wellness to sickness.

I came from a background of humorous people extending back several generations. Using humor as a sixth sense while in life's waiting room has enriched my life. To live without humor is to win without getting the prize. I am so thankful for inheriting the humor gene. Thanks to all my relatives for sharing their memories with me. The decision to finally write this book came after meeting a new friend, Carolyn Winstead Bagley. We met while she was recovering from surgery. All I had to do was mention that I had written a few stories and was thinking of writing a book. She immediately started encouraging me to put my idea into action. Also a big thanks to my friend of many years, Dwight Link for sharing his talent in the illustrations used. I graciously appreciate Marie Harris Pridgen, one of the busiest women I know, for her expertise in editing my work. This task would not have been possible without the help of my friend, Kayla Kelley, whose sharp computer skills shaped my work into book form. A big thanks to my wonderful daughter-in-law, Mitzi Huff for the priceless photography that light up my stories.

I hope you will enjoy my reflections on life as I knew it for the past sixty- plus years. Thanks to all the church groups, clubs, and especially seniors, who invited me to share vignettes of my life. All of you have become a part of my past and my future. For those of you who find your name in this book, please know that you left a smile and a great memory in my heart.

Introduction

(1949-2018)

The stories I have shared reflect my life growing up in the country in a large family as a tenant farmer's daughter. They are snap-shots, sprinkled with humor, of various activities and experiences. With being a farmer's daughter, comes an appreciation for the value of things that matter: meaningful relationships, the love between brothers and sisters who share so much in common, and great memories made. My Daddy's shadow and his influence on my life, can be seen in most of them. I treasure the memories and appreciate the opportunities afforded me to learn real life values, a sound work ethic and the love of family. Those who missed living life in the country, have bypassed many opportunities to gain wisdom and common sense. I will consider my efforts worthwhile if readers gain a nugget or two about the benefits of country living while in life's waiting room. Putting my thoughts and memories into this book, has reinforced the importance of leaving a legacy behind that might encourage my successors to hope for the best and to bloom where planted.

Adjusting my sail to circumstances both past and present can be credited to the exposure to difficult times years ago. Now I know they were only mild challenges that shaped my ability to see the humor in life events. Every day is truly a gift from our Creator and what we do with it is our gift back to him. Spend time with your loved ones and share a story or two while they are with you. Pass on what you have learned with your family and friends. We all need encouragement and inspiration from others. Choosing to write a book is a great avenue for sharing our experiences with those whom we are yet to meet. We are all more alike than we are different.

Snapshots From A Country Diary

Sprinkled With Humor

TENANT FARMING AND MORE THROUGH THE LENS OF A FARMER'S DAUGHTER

Tenant farming, also known as sharecropping, was a way of making a living on a farm by relinquishing part of the cash crop, which was tobacco, to the landowner/landlord. We were fortunate enough to only give one fourth of the tobacco income back to the landlord instead of half. Back in the forties and fifties, workers in other fields of labor might wonder what happened when the tobacco money ran out. Daddy often said, if it was a good year, pay day came in early fall, and the money was already owed, leaving very little to live on until the next spring. Options for money making were quite limited, often a calf, pig, or wheat was sold for income. Of course, money was only spent on necessities back then. There were no phones, no newspapers, and no magazines coming in the mail box at our house. News was learned from talking with neighbors at the nearest country store around a wood- burning stove. The men called it "chewing the fat." The women learned news from quilting parties held in individual homes. Mama was always telling that she was pregnant again. The ladies kept up-to- date on who had a streak of bad luck, what vegetables were canned, and who moved in or out of the neighborhood.

Sharecroppers were known for helping their neighbors,

especially during hard times, which was the usual: families losing their home to a fire, tragedies involving children, and acute illnesses taking the life of family members. To borrow from ones' neighbors was very common. Women would gather as much garden crops as possible, saving all they could put in jars for the upcoming winter. A favorite memory is Mama sending me to a neighbor to borrow the canner, which is a large enamel pot with a lid and rack used to process the vegetables. Lois was very busy with her own large family. When asked about borrowing her canner, she replied, "I'm so sorry, David is taking a bath in it right now." I waited a while and carried the canner home with me. In those days of living in the country, it was the norm to use items for multiple uses. Without indoor bathrooms and modern conveniences we have today, families learned to make do with what they had.

Going into town occurred about twice monthly, only for necessities, food, material for making clothes, and "bound to have medicines." There were no shelves full of medicine bottles like we have today. There was one small bottle of merthiolate for cuts and scrapes. Our neighbor, Aunt Gracie, always kept a bottle on a shelf for use by the neighborhood children. If a window pane was accidentally broken out, someone had to give up their pillow to stuff the hole. Now I see empty window panes in fast food places for the decorative effect. In fact, when I moved into my new home in 1997, I found an old window and designed the empty holes for a bathroom that had no real window. I had no idea I would use that idea fifty years later. We had plastic curtains, that stayed ragged because we pulled on them constantly. Mama often pinned her needles in them, way up high where we couldn't reach them. That was the best way she had of keeping up with the needle. She didn't have a sewing box full of stuff.

If I or any of my siblings was observed wasting anything, the scolding surely followed. Some of the more frequent reasons included putting more than two eggs in a cake, using too much lard to fry a chicken, holding the refrigerator door open too long, and having too much flour left in the pan after making biscuits. I try hard to watch such things these days. Remember, a woman can waste more with a tablespoon, than a man can haul in with a wheelbarrow. All family members used one bath pan. If one of us was caught leaving the cake of soap in the bottom of the pan, it was considered a misdemeanor. All of us were reminded of how much things cost and how limited our resources were. My three sisters and I were so happy to receive a real beauty salon hair dryer on a stand, from our Dear Aunt Dorothy. We were known for being meticulous about our hair, which continues to this day. After getting it up and in use for the first time, Ma ma went outside the house to see how much faster the power meter wheel was turning. Most of the time, she thought it was going too fast and taking too much electricity. I rarely use a hair dryer now, but I enjoy having no restrictions. We learned to be resourceful as there was no money for extra primping devices, make-up, etc. I looked forward to Daddy coming home from the store with a brown paper bag. I cut the bag into one inch strips five inches long. I wrapped my hair around the paper and twisted both ends together. I was so pleased to have nice curls to show off at school the next day. The little wads of paper did not bother me as I slept, but today I cannot tolerate a cotton ball in my hair at night. In my adult years, I have considered using the paper strips again, going to the Mall, maybe catching the attention of some millennials. Perhaps, they could save money and get attention from such a fad, getting something started. Surely, they are concerned about reducing the cost of hair care these days.

One of my fondest memories relates to the baking of a cake for the annual Berea School Halloween Carnival. I was about twelve years old, not quite old enough to bake a normal looking cake. I wanted so badly to be able to take a cake to school that would be entered in the cake walk game. Since we kept cocoa as a regular staple, I decided to make a chocolate cake. We did not own an electric mixer. After much guessing at ingredients and adding extra flour to make the cake stay together, I produced a cake that was so heavy, I could barely lift it. Off to school the next day with the cake. The lady in charge of the cake walk was the sweetest, kindest, and most gentle soul in the Berea community, Mrs.

Margaret Adcock. She accepted my cake with such a loving spirit; I know she did not want to hurt my feelings. I might add that she was no kin to me. She did not have the heart to tell me my cake did not qualify. Her daughter, Peggy, was one of my classmates. I vaguely remember the music playing and adults stopping on certain numbers. As I anxiously sat in the auditorium, I heard my cake, #21 called out, asking the winner to come forward. I felt like a million dollars. It just so happened that my neighbor, Emma Jane Sherman, was the lucky winner. When she returned to her seat with the cake, I heard her say, "This is the heaviest, blackest , most lopsided cake I have ever seen." I started to laugh hysterically. Bless her heart, she went to her grave without knowing I made the cake. I think I will tell her children about this memorable event. Without sounding too proud, I can honestly say that today, my chocolate cakes get rave reviews from some of the best cooks. A few years ago, I won a blue ribbon from the church I grew up in for my chocolate cake. The judge was Sheila Williams, who knew me quite well. We remain friends today, and she is also a retired nurse, enjoying life on her farm.

Earlier, I alluded to the money running out and the limited resources for earning more money. Most large farms have a nice creek meandering through the property. Having a creek is ideal for locating a whiskey making outfit, better known as a liquor still. Finding good homemade whiskey (white lightning) was a bit of a challenge in those days, especially for the quality Daddy was known for making. Having nice clean glass jars on hand was a must. My wrists are so small and just right for washing jars. Plans don't always run smoothly for this kind of operation. People talk and often to the wrong people. They didn't always mind their own business. If someone saw Daddy buying more than ten pounds of sugar, word was spread around about their suspicions. This included everyone who was at the store and finally included the Revenue folks in town, fourteen miles away. The operation was up and running before we had company from town. That day is most memorable. One week-day morning, the revenue guys entered our house, where they found me churning, Geneva making biscuits, and Mama washing clothes. The younger children were running about the house playing with their home-made toys. Sure enough, they stopped me from churning, looked into the buttermilk, looked in the flour chest, and into the cook stove where a blackberry cobbler was baking. It is no telling how hungry those guys were. We all got tickled but stayed on task. Besides, I like to look at guys in uniform with special patches and emblems. They were certainly designed differently than bib overalls. I sure hope those guys got smarter over the years. Maybe it was their first assignment in the County. When Daddy came in for the noon meal, he cordially greeted them. After not being able to find any whiskey inside our house, they decided to venture outside the house. There was an old winding path leading to the old house, where we once lived. Under a large oak tree, was an old beat up car, with three cases of white lightning in the trunk. (see illustration) They walked on by and decided to go back to town without any evidence. What a wasted day for them. We talked about this at the lunch table, enjoying biscuits, cobbler, fresh buttermilk, peas, and corn on the cob. Beware, there were later visits, ending with plenty of evidence. Our winter survival money was threatened, not money for spending on a cruise. Sixty years later, feature articles on whiskey making operations are available. I bet Daddy could give them some good advice on perfecting the recipe.

Entertainment was homespun. Most neighborhoods had at least one pony and a pony cart. Riding the pony cart was something to look forward to on the week-ends, as work was a priority during the week. My oldest sister Geneva was thrown from the cart one Saturday afternoon because of a reckless driver. She never rode one again. Girls made play houses in the woods, using old leftover items for make believe furniture. We painted our nails with pokeberry juice. The boys went swimming in the ford of the river, often taking a bath when the water was clear. Fishing with homemade poles and tackle was a favorite past time. Because of the isolation in rural areas, we really didn't know much about what was going on in the world. The adults met on a neighbor's porch in the summertime to talk about their tobacco, how bad times were, and how badly they needed rain for the crops. They always thought the year they were in was the worst. The year I recall Daddy talking of the most was 1953. No one made any money that year because of a prolonged drought. He said the next year was not much better. We would often return home, finding fresh tire tracks in the dirt. Daddy knew it was his younger brother Billy because he was the only one who could afford tires with enough tread to leave tracks. My first trip to see Christmas lights in town at night was to Oxford, North Carolina. The landlord's daughter Ree, stopped by to take me. She would drive me to other special occasions' treating me like a baby sister. I now call her "Sister." I remember asking her what kept the curtains from catching on fire from those burning candles. We laugh about this now as well as other situations she knew about. This wonderful woman we called Ree saw all eight of us grow up, followed us with our problems, successes, illnesses, marriages, and luck, be it good or bad. One night as a five- year- old child, I forced a ring from a flashlight assembly onto my finger. Daddy could not get it off, so he walked about a half mile to the landlord's house. Ree took me to Oxford to Dr. Clay's house late in the night. Dr. and Mrs. Clay used a nail file to remove the metal ring. I no longer force rings of any kind on my fingers. There is one thing for certain, not one of us was ever taken to the Doctor because we swallowed money.

Having nice clothes meant a lot to me back then. Most of my clothes came from a hand-me down pile. Now I know that clothes are only reflections of the latest fashions and do not define who we are. Being comfortable in my own skin is much better than owning a Chesterfield coat, something I badly wanted in high school. This was a popular coat that all the city girls wore. More than fifty years later, I have a closet full of coats, but at least I understand why I have so many. I must admit I have gotten past the coat ordeal. However, it does not stop me from dressing up today, and at times, being overdressed for the occasion.

The dating scene was narrowed down to persons in the immediate community or acquaintances of your older siblings. We did not hang out, a term our teenagers call dating today. We were not allowed to be at home with our date if our parents were not present. Our parents felt it necessary to know your date's parents and their entire ancestry. General questions were directed towards their work background. And concerning the date; did he have common sense, did he arise early in the morning, preferably before the rooster crowed. Of course, in a small community, everybody knew almost all they needed to know about other people. Word of mouth was viewed as rather reliable. What wasn't true was passed on as the truth. I vividly knew of a situation in which the Mother bragged about her son, because she desperately wanted to get rid of him. Later on, we all had a good understanding of why she used this tactic.

How did we know where we would be living the next year? In the fall of each year, if the landlord told the sharecropper to sow his turnip salad patch, that meant he would be staying on the farm, farming it another year. It was unusual for a family to live on the same farm for forty plus years. We lived in three different houses during those forty years. Each move brought us more room and a better house. Eviction notices were not used in those days, not out in the country. I so much enjoy having my own salad patch on my own land with no strings attached. When I sow it each year, that memory returns of what it meant years ago. I enjoy inviting my city friends, especially Maxine and Mussette, to come help themselves. We have great conversations while in the salad patch. It is such a great opportunity to share my relationship with the land with my friends. Daddy always invited neighbors, who did not have a patch, to pick from his. Again, this provided a great opportunity to hear the latest news of the community. Often, grapevine news originated in the turnip salad patch.

Daddy was never one to avoid working on special holidays if he felt he had something important to do. He would even kill hogs on Christmas Eve. One year, he decided to move to the former landlord's house on a cold rainy day before Christmas. Most of the manpower available to help was already indulging in the "spirits." Moving was quite different then, no real packing going on, resulting in things being thrown onto a long flat trailer, pulled by a tractor. There were a few trucks in the neighborhood. The heaviest item to be moved, a coppertone brown refrigerator, ended up on the back end of the trailer, almost on the edge. Going up a steep, slicky red mud hill, with a refrigerator tilting back and forth, held on by two skinny men, caused a lot of grief. (see illustration) Finally, the trailer arrived at the kitchen door, all contents intact. Mama missed most of the excitement, as she was in a car holding on to the one item she wanted to protect, her Daddy's mantel clock. Of all the items moved, the clock is still in the family collectibles. Most of the men who helped move that day are no longer around to talk about it. I think poor people might have better luck. They learn how to make do with very few resources, while tending to lend a helping hand.

There were many odd happenings in the Landlord's house. I was married and away from home, missing the last move. My youngest sister, Beatrice (Bea) was so happy to have her own bedroom. Unlike the other houses, it had an indoor bathroom. One night she heard a loud howling noise coming from her bedroom window. The deep breathing sounded like some kind of animal. She started screaming, awakening Daddy in the wee hours of the morning. Upon entering her room, he saw a large cow rubbing against the outside wall of the house. With a lifetime of dealing with cows, he knew how to get the cow away from the

house. On another occasion in Bea's bedroom, she heard a strange
noise coming from the floor. One must imagine what something
scaly sounds like on a linoleum rug. This type of rug is very cold
in the winter and stiff. The surface is very smooth. Again, she
screamed and called for Daddy. He came in to see a long black
snake slithering along the floor. Needless to say, he killed the
snake, which had crawled in through an opening in the porch
screen door. I think the hole was wired together as it would have
been very expensive to rescreen the whole door. These are two
episodes that I know of, but Bea probably has many more to share.

I would be remiss if I didn't mention tobacco. We had small
tobacco crops, not over 15 acres in a year. However, this was
considered a lot back then. We were lucky to get it planted and
saved with help that was available. My brothers would help other
farmers in return for their help, known as bartering. I learned to tie
tobacco the old fashioned way, on a stick fitted on a wooden stand.
In the later years, Daddy bought a tobacco tying machine. There
were real problems. My sister Jo Ann had the skills necessary to
keep it running. Since moving to Java, I have learned that tying a
bow at the end of the stick, was not used in this area. I can still tie
that bow today. We tied it this way because this method required
less tobacco thread. A barn was considered 500 sticks. Harvesting
one barn a day and two for the week was average. Daddy was a
successful tobacco farmer. He knew how to prepare the land for a
good crop. He was also very skilled at curing tobacco. The goal
was to grow good tobacco that would yield weight. More weight
meant a bigger check at the market. So many steps have been
removed from the entire tobacco occupation, but the end product is
the same. Farmers can now have larger crops. An entire book can
be written on tobacco from the small plant to the pack of cigarettes
on the store shelf. I don't believe tobacco will ever cease to exist.
I remain interested in tobacco, and enjoy seeing it grow in the
fields. There are very successful tobacco farmers in the Java
community. The Ragsdale brothers and the Gregorys are real pros
on growing tobacco. I don't miss rubbing the hard, black sticky
wax off my hands, the hot days in the sun, and the worry I saw

Daddy go through when the rain did not come. Temporary situations teach us that better times are in the making. Farm life brought its joy in so many other ways. The things I missed on the farm were not all that important. However, the lessons learned are valuable and remain with me. I have attempted to reflect some memories into a song, "Tobacco Farmer's Daughter." Perhaps some day, some artist will think its worth singing about. Because Loretta Lynn is my hero, I subconsciously hum it to the tune of her signature song, "Coal Miners Daughter." In my research of her life, I note that she, too, was one of eight children and her Daddy also sold a hog for cash money. We must never forget where we came from. We must keep a vision of where we want to go in life. We must appreciate the value of having good neighbors, fresh food, a great country church, and friendships made in difficult circumstances. Without those experiences, we are unable to

complete the mission we have been given by our Creator. Develop opportunities to hear somebody's story. People need to know you care and are interested in them. Ride out to the country on a warm sunny day and find where the sign on that old tobacco barn by the side of the road came from. Take pictures of your homeplace house before it falls down. Try to remember the location of the clothes line, the garden where you picked purple hull peas, and the rose bush you planted by the old well.

Tobacco Farmer's Daughter
By: Faye A. Little

Well I was born a Tobacco Farmer's daughter
In a tenant house on a farm in Carolina

We were poor but we didn't know it
Daddy was too proud to ever show it

My Daddy worked all day in the tobacco field
All night long down at the liquor still

The clothes we wore won't in style
Coming from the hand- me- down pile

Daddy loved and raised eight kids on a farmer's pay
Mama cut our hair and loved us in her own way

In the summer time, we'd all go berry picking
And in the winter time, we'd pick a few chickens

The old house it still stands
Surrounded by weeds and old tin cans

Oh, it was good to be a Tobacco Farmer's daughter
I treasure those memories and I oughta

All the work was low pay
Come another year, on that farm we'd stay

All those years have come and gone
And it's good just to go back home

To see those tobacco barns
Where all my memories belong

In Carolina on that tobacco farm

The Chicken House Returns
(Spring 1993)

Years ago, people didn't pay much attention to how close adjacent out buildings were to the living quarters. Out buildings on a farm, might include the smokehouse where meat was cured and stored, a tool shed for frequently used tools, or a well house that was built around a dug well. Remember, no one lived close enough to have city water. By the early forties, indoor plumbing became a luxury. As the years go by, we often start noticing our surroundings more, becoming motivated to make things look better. In the process we tend to discard possessions seeing them as no longer necessary in our lives. The art of raising chickens in the back yard in a chicken house begin to be outdated. Chicken was the one meat that most country folk could afford to have on hand.

This was the case with Daddy's chicken house. I cannot recall the time when Daddy did not have chickens "on the yard" and a chicken house. "On the yard" meant the chickens were free to roam, scratch, hop up on the porch, and entertain us. In the Summer of 1993, my oldest brother, Sambo, who owned the property, made an observation. The chicken house was just too close to the house. In fact, when the wind came from the right direction, an offensive odor came right across the front porch of the house. In the country, this is usually not a deal breaker. After all, there were only five or six chickens roaming around.

Therefore, a major project got underway. The chicken house was dismantled and the birds were given away to various people Daddy knew. The reference to birds reflects what my Uncle Jonah called chickens, "gospel birds." The task was a bit harder than first imagined, as it was made of hand hewn logs with nice notches cut out from oak wood that could withstand high winds and storms and a tin top. The rich ammonia soil beneath was quickly converted to a garden spot where I later planted holly hock seeds. Their blooms were huge and bright. We quickly accepted that there would be no baby chicks in the spring of 1993.

As time passed, Daddy kept talking about how much he missed his chickens. By word of mouth, Daddy was told by a close neighbor where he could get two grown roosters. They arrived and were placed in two old wooden boxes nailed to the side of the wood shed, which was further from the house. Getting them all comfortable and happy was a great challenge for Daddy. The roosters loved to be petted. You would have to know my Daddy to appreciate the funny remarks he made about the behavior of those roosters, all hemmed up in a box with nothing to crow about. He finally decided that they just could not be themselves in such a restricted environment. The decision to build a new chicken house was put into action. A retired neighbor and Daddy worked a week building a new chicken pen and house. Daddy wanted them to be able to roam around in the daytime and to retreat to the house at night. Too, he was very worried about wild animals harming them. He decided to locate it near the woods, under the shade trees, a good distance from his living quarters. The new chicken shelter was ready for occupancy the first week in June. Word got out in the neighborhood about the ordeal and his friends came to share in the event. I remember walking with him to the wooded area to see this new chicken habitat and how excited he was to talk about all the details.

There are some funny anecdotal notes about this ordeal than can best be told by Daddy. For example, just how does a rooster act when he has lived in a two by two foot cell and suddenly gets placed among eight hens in a brand new place? Needless to say, the chickens were no happier than their owner. We should all think about how decisions we make might affect the livelihood of other people, even if it involves a chicken. It is no telling how many miles Daddy walked back and forth to that chicken house, racking up much needed exercise. It was a place to sit in the shade, watch the chickens, and reminisce about years gone by. He enjoyed taking his visitors to that special place. Children need to know what it means for a chicken "to steal a nest." I doubt that this term can be answered by modern technology of today. The hen would quietly find a very remote out of sight place, such as a brush pile, or under an old pile of wood, lay her eggs and hatch baby chicks. It is my hope that chicken houses will remain in our back yards and that we can find such a place to be still, appreciating years gone by.

I plan to go very soon to visit my cousin, Bobbie, who has gotten into the chicken business just like Daddy did. He would be so proud to know the tradition is alive and well in the family and in the community of Berea, North Carolina, where he lived most of his life. To further etch this story in my mind, I recently created a memorial area with various statutes of chickens on the ground outside my office window. I enjoy telling my country friends how the idea surfaced. It keeps the memory alive. As I visit yard and estate sales, my eyes are on the look out for chickens. My son Jason has mentioned the idea of getting some real chickens, once he gets settled in. He, too, has fond memories of chickens "on the yard." In the meantime, let us not take for granted the things in this world that have meaning; may we treasure them and pass on our fondness for them to our families. Don't wait for the eulogy and the smell of fresh dirt.

Snapshots From A Country Diary

Sprinkled With Humor

The Puttin Pan Episode

(The Summer of 1966)

I was a junior in high School and a great admirer of my Home Economics teacher, Mrs. Frances Boyd. I was always telling Ma ma what Mrs. Boyd said on various topics. I think she finally got to not wanting to hear much about the lady. "Home Make" teachers tend to want to know a bit more about family dynamics than they are able to learn just from seeing the student in a school setting. I was quite close to Mrs. Boyd, as she would call on me to do small tasks for her. At this time in my life, I now know she was giving me validation, which greatly enhanced my self esteem. The day came when she wanted to make a home visit to my house out in the country.

I had alerted Mama that Mrs. Boyd was coming on a certain evening about 3 p.m., mainly because I would be off the bus and at home. Teenagers did not have their own personal cars to drive to and from school. We all rode the bus. I did not tell Daddy about the visit. I worried about the visit, wondering if the house would be in order, would the floor be swept, and would my youngest brother, Jerry, be crying. In fact, there were five children younger than me. What would Mrs. Boyd think about the house, and what if she needed to use the bathroom? Would she just delay everything to avoid going to the outhouse behind the hog pen?

The day finally came on a hot, summer day. The flies were inside as the screens were full of holes with no air conditioning in a cinderblock house. A house made with cement block walls tended to hold heat. We probably could have fried an egg on the walls because of the heat. We were accustomed to having something to eat as soon as we got off the bus and into the kitchen. There was a door separating the kitchen from the "front room." Front rooms in tenant houses had to serve dual purposes. They served as parlors when dating age arrived, sleeping space for siblings, and visitors. When Mrs. Boyd arrived, I offered her a seat in the front room and closed the door to the kitchen.

The conversation slowly started and the noise in the kitchen accelerated. I knew what the noise was. Children did not sit in chairs; instead we sat on a long wooden bench. It was rare in those days to have a table with matching chairs. The five siblings were up on the table, each with a metal spoon, banging in that puttin pan. All of a sudden, I heard Daddy come in the back door to the kitchen. Very sternly and loudly, he hollered out, "Get down off that table out of that darn putting pan before I whip all of you." At that moment, all I could hear was the sound of metal spoons being thrown into that puttin pan and feet jumping to the floor, not in unison. Not one of them came into the front room but Daddy did. When he opened the door, he looked right at Mrs. Boyd, extended his hand, and welcomed her to our house. Mrs. Boyd was so poised and lady like in every way.

The visit ended on a good note. I am curious to this day, wondering if she entered some kind of note on my school record. After fifty- two years, I am not worried about such things. It is amazing that now I know what the visit was about and that all families have special dynamics. Is there a child in the city or in the country that has a fresh- baked, blackberry cobbler with berries picked on the farm waiting on the table for an after- school snack? I doubt it. There is no use for a front room anymore, as dating at home has gone out of style, very little visiting is done, and families are much smaller, no longer needing to sleep in the "front room." Newer homes have living rooms that are empty. The teenagers certainly are not sitting on a sofa talking about Saturday night Hee Haw jokes.

Mrs. Boyd had a great influence on my life as a teenager. Among many things, she taught me how to sew, how to make a pie crust, and how to set a pretty table for company. If she observed one of her students patting cream potatoes flat, ten points were deducted from their grade. She dwelled on presenting food in an appetizing manner. I learned later that she did not have a daughter. She made me feel special and guided me through some of the social graces that I would not have learned otherwise. I have followed much of her advice to this day. Maybe I should bake a blackberry cobbler and invite her to visit. In fact, I don't believe Home Economics is on school curriculums now. Maybe someday, some school committee will advocate for its return. I strongly feel that male students should have the opportunity to sign up for the course. We should never be hesitant to talk about where we came from and our hopes for the future. It is the past that has shaped us for the road ahead. For that, I am so appreciative and grateful.

A WORD TO THE WISE IF YOU ARE A WOMAN CONTEMPLATING MARRYING A FOREST SERVICE MAN

(Summer, 1988)

While enjoying an afternoon visit with the wives of three Forest Service men, it occurred to us that we should write down some interesting facts to consider about this particular sampling of men and their jobs. This conversation transpired around 1988, one year before I married my Ed. I have found all of the information to be very credible. (Contributors Laverne Hobgood (Charles) Pat Sykes (Ed), and Catherine Ingram (Jimmy).

If you are contemplating marrying a Forest Service Man, you must be willing to:

- Spend more time washing clothes because by their nature, they love to get dirty from head to toe.

- Keep supper warm because they usually get fire calls around 4:55 pm.

- Go to your social functions alone because their day off is perfect for fishing and hunting anything that moves.

- Run the vacuum cleaner around fifteen to twenty pairs of shoes scattered all over the house because they must wear certain ones depending on the weather.

- Mend his clothes because they tear them up in all the rough places they venture into, not limited to woods, caves, rivers, rock piles, brush piles, etc.

- Have smoky sex after they return from all fires, reason unknown.

- Receive multiple phone calls after 6 pm, because they don't talk about their jobs at work.

- Keep a white sheet available at all times for de-ticking them from March through December.

- Learn basic first aid because they get cut, fall in creeks, get eyes poked by tree limbs, skin up their legs, as they are not hurt bad enough to go to the doctor.

- Learn the skills of removing beggar lice from his cap to his shoes unless you want to pick it off the other clothes in the washing machine.

- Lastly, go with him to all the retirement parties and funerals, after all they were pretty good fellows.

Without further explanation, it takes a special woman to manage such a man, but I am in my 28th year and still learning. I guess it would be inappropriate to post this important information on E- Harmony or other dating sites. We ladies agree that times have changed and are willing to revise this listing should it become necessary. Words cannot describe how much laughter ensued this afternoon among three of my great friends. I regret that one of my friends, Pat Sykes, is no longer with us, however, her great sense of humor remains.

As I settled in as being secretary to a Forest Service man, I soon came up with some humorous ways to handle the frequent calls at all times of the day, twenty-four- seven. This really was more appropriate after Ed became a Consultant Forester. The calls really increased then. I tried to get him to let me put the following on the answering machine, and he would not agree, said it was not professional.

Hello.........you have reached Ed and Andy's secretary hotline!

Please follow these instructions:

1. If you are calling to complain about a logger, press 1.
2. If you are calling to report beetles in your trees press 2.
3. If you are calling to reject a bid you were offered, press 3
4. If you are calling to tell them you have money for them, you can reach them immediately via mobile phone.

Otherwise, call back tomorrow; they are very busy and the secretary is not on the pay roll.   Thanks!

FLY AND I
(Winter 2002)

It was a sunny cold day in February 2002 when I had the opportunity to meet a friend of a lifetime. We had white pine trees growing on the farm that could be seen from the road that would be future Christmas trees. A nice couple came to our house and approached Ed about buying some of these trees. He replied, "Only if you dig them up yourselves." They readily accepted his suggestion. I decided it was so cold and raw that day, that they just might enjoy some hot coffee. I was excited about meeting somebody new in this new neighborhood where we had relocated. Margaret and Larry accepted my offer to come inside to warm and to have coffee. I did not know at the time that she liked coffee. They came inside, the conversation never stopped. She and I talked gardening and planting shrubs. They planned to use the white pines as part of their landscape at their new home. I immediately knew I was getting a friend forever. Margaret and I stayed in touch, and eventually we formed our own garden club,

"Country Cousins of Java." The club included Fly, her brother, Jesse Barksdale, Marie Harris, and Rochelle Lee. We visited nurseries, planned our own garden shows, and shared our garden tricks of the trade.

After becoming well acquainted, we started going to special gardening events. I learned of the annual Virginia Lily Show, scheduled in Chatham, Virginia. We discussed going and what to wear. We both decided we should dress up in our linen dresses. After all, we didn't want to go underdressed or tacky. One never knows where genuine Southern Belles might show up. We arrived at the Church to find beautiful lilies on display everywhere. It was very well organized in a beautiful church. We mixed in the crowd slowly and quietly. Soon we were asking questions, reading labels, and acting like real southern belles. Suddenly Margaret turned to me saying, "Faye, I feel like a fly in a glass of buttermilk." We have laughed over and over about this expression. Communication had never been so clear. I thought she was looking around at the lilies, but she was looking to see if she was in fact, the only black guest. From that day on she became my friend, "Fly." We love it and we treasure the threads woven in our friendship. Our fifteen- year friendship has been wonderful. I never expected a fly to bring me so much cheer. It was so worth getting up for that morning to enjoy the great experience God had in store for us. We have shared our childhood memories, our family dynamics, and our journeys.

Most of all, we discovered how much we have in common. I am looking forward to adding more notes to my friendship journal. When we all learn that we are more alike than we are different, our friendship list will multiply greatly. I hope the beautiful pomegranate tree is still by the sidewalk near the church. We must have stood there a half hour admiring it. We both purchased one for our gardens. This is what serious gardening friends do.

Uncle Ben's Ride on Tweetsie

1980

Don't overlook your kinfolk when wanting to hear some good humor. My late sister Jo Ann gave our family a very accurate account of what happened that fall day almost forty years ago. Having the opportunity to leave Granville County on a pleasure trip did not occur very often for a number of reasons. One being, finding someone to be the designated driver in the event alcohol was involved. After all, the sign that hung on his kitchen wall surely represented his beliefs about booze.

"I have read so much about the bad effects of smoking, eating, drinking, and sex, that I have decided to give up reading."

The decision to take the trip would be a fun day for Uncle Ben, Jo Ann, and Dolly. They arrived at Tweetsie Railroad just in time for the ride on the train. Uncle Ben sat alone, and his wife and Jo Ann sat near the back, in a great spot to observe. All was going smoothly until the robbery reenactment by the Indians started. No one knew their tickets would buy them extra unrehearsed entertainment before a live audience. Jo Ann noticed that Uncle Ben became very agitated and restless. Now, it was a well-known fact that he had indeed, drank enough to be relaxed but not enough to pass out.   As the Indians got closer to his seat, he stood up, sticking his hands down into his striped bib overalls, likely for his pocketknife, that was always razor sharp. The Adcocks never carried dull pocket knives. Jo Ann could hear him say, "You ain't going to take my money." It was then she realized he really thought he was about to be robbed. People were laughing hysterically. His wife was yelling, "Sit down you fool!" Finally Jo Ann was able to get to his seat, getting him calmed down. The actors jumped off the train faster than they got on. There is no way the actors could have known they would encounter such a situation. Perhaps, they all received an award for such fine acting. I wish I could have interviewed them for their rendition of the event. They certainly deserved one. It was time to return home to familiar surroundings on US Hwy.158 in northern Granville County. The crowd who frequented his house often, patiently waited for their arrival to hear all about the trip. Uncle Ben's house was often referred to as the "watering hole" for the community. All people were welcomed, fed, and entertained free of charge. The cook-outs were attended by people of all ages and backgrounds.   There is nothing left of the house except a cracked well house, driven into by a cousin who had impaired vision. My brother owns the property now. Many a tale can be quickly repeated by the surviving kin, mostly cousins.

Jo Ann had much fun telling this story back home. He never wanted to ride Tweetsie again.   However, if we fast forward about thirty years, it is normal to expect to be robbed most any place any time. It is debatable as to whether or not the whiskey influenced his reaction. At any rate, it is a good story for us to laugh about well into this century.

Women On The Job in Rural America (The Nineties)

Sharing some of my observations of working women in rural areas I have traveled, reflects much that has changed over the years. I am very concerned that the next generation will think it has always been that way. They will not know the role of women from the previous generation. Mothers used to stay at home, raise their children, prepare meals from their gardens, and do all the housework. The men worked outside, taking care of the yard, doing the heavy work. I want them to appreciate the sacrifices of the previous generation of women and the changing roles that evolved. Women rarely had time for themselves. They put the needs of their children and husbands first. Most of the big decisions were made by the man of the house, ie, how money was spent, what major purchases were made, etc. I have recognized my failure to thank them for their contributions and efforts they made to make it easier for me. Most of my observations reflect changing roles in the country sides, particularly outside work. Women are now mowing their own yards. They can be seen wearing hard hats on construction jobs, driving big semi-trucks, and operating heavy equipment. It is interesting to note that women have transitioned into more jobs involving hard manual labor, that used to be common only on the farms where they were the jobs performed by men. I won't detail the events of how and why this has happened. Perhaps, that can be better explained at the next garden party on the porch at my house in Java.

While in route to the small quaint town of Chatham, Virginia, I had the opportunity to observe a situation not all that common these days. It was still cool enough for a morning fire. I looked to my right, just outside the city limits, to see a lady in her forties, swinging an axe, chopping wood. She was in a long night gown with a cloth band wrapped around her head. I think the axe was a bit dull, as she was using a lot of force. The chopping block was located very close to the back door of the house. The wood was cut into short sticks, that were likely used in a wood cook stove or some type of stove that used short sticks. Having a chopping block close by was surely in her favor, as she was probably the person who did it all. I did not see any stacked wood which made me believe she just did it from day to day as needed. Maybe she was waiting for a man to come home. She saw me and nodded her head. It would have surely been interesting to hear the rest of the story. I regret that I did not stop to chat. I never had to chop wood as the men in my life owned this task.

In my home community near Oxford, North Carolina, I had to stop for road construction work. A woman was holding the stop and go sign, wearing a hard hat, boots, and a backpack. The temperature that day hovered around 100 degrees. She was the only female among a crew of eight men. She was smiling as if she was happy to be holding the sign. My first thoughts were about the bathroom situation. There on sight was a port-a-john on the back of a truck. Maybe this was the only job available as unemployment is high in this area. Nevertheless, she was doing the job, despite what I perceived as stress in its highest degree. Again, talking to her would have been interesting, no doubt. Was this a choice or was it out of necessity to keep a roof over her head? Mama's cousin Bill, once said," need will knock at your door, but when bound to have knocks, there are no choices left." I have lived long enough to know the difference between the two.

On entering another small town, Roxboro, North Carolina, I passed a small country church with a large lawn and cemetery. A lady was mowing the lawn and a second lady using a weed eater, trimming around the head stones. There were no men seen. Perhaps these two ladies owned their business or were from the congregation. They were handling the equipment easier than I can run my Kitchen Aid mixer. I doubt they were worried about a time clock. It reminded me to be thankful for a nicely manicured church lawn and cemetery. A few years ago, I would not have imagined women assuming this role. However, the women of small country churches have always been very attentive to how the church looks on the inside and out. They are quick to note when repairs are needed. They will speak up at meetings, not afraid to voice these concerns. They will go even further and have bake sales to pay for repairs. Since then, I have seen more women performing yard maintenance in the same manner.

As we travel about this wonderful country, may we not overlook these dedicated hard- working women who are providing a great service, improving our environments and adding beauty to our landscapes. Take the opportunity to thank them for their contributions in a time of uncertainty, low wages, and extreme weather conditions, among many other hidden obstacles. They deserve recognition for their willingness to undertake these jobs. My observations are only about three women, but there are many more out there. The next time you observe one in a non-traditional role, show appreciation for the positive impact she has made in your world. As for the rest of us, we can always bake a pound cake for our new neighbor, take a friend to the doctor, or make a flower pot for a shut-in. Even better, sit down and chat with them. We can learn from their rich past, their journeys, and their unrealized dreams. We all need encouragement and validation. I recently was waiting for the shuttle bus to take me to a nearby hospital to visit my brother Jerry. In a very soft, gentle voice, a lady asked me to sit beside her while she waited for the bus. As soon as she spoke, I knew she was someone whom I worked with twenty- one years ago. It was a moment to remember; we hugged and just kept talking. I plan to get back with Harriet very soon. We both want to discuss all that has happened between 1997 and 2018.

Gardening and More

(1997-2018)

Gardening has been so much a part of my life that I would be remiss if I did not mention some of my experiences. Coming from a background of hard workers, nature lovers, and a love for the outside, certainly pointed me straight to the ground.

I loved planting seeds since a small child. My dream was to have a flower garden large enough for making my own flower pots. Indeed, this has happened. When I moved to Java, Virginia, there was great space for a garden. An old tobacco pack barn was near our house. My first plan involved making the garden as an attachment to the barn. No tobacco barn should stand alone. Ed was quite lenient in letting me plant any place on the farm.

I made many mistakes, mainly being in too big of a hurry to get every foot of space occupied. I accepted all and any plants given me. I failed to ask intelligent questions, ie, does this plant become invasive. I have spent more time and hard work removing plants that I no longer wanted in my garden. Of course, in doing so, the soil got tilled often. Please, if you must give your friend some mint, tell them to confine it to a large pot, as it will multiply like rabbits. I bought gardening books, special tools, and anything sold in a bag labeled for gardeners.

My garden soon blossomed, having shrubs, perennials, annuals, and climbing plants. I started to feel that somebody needed to see the fruits of my labor. I planned porch garden parties. My great gardening friend, Fly, was doing the same thing with her garden. In looking back, I see much competition going on. I had a close city friend, Anne Michie to visit occasionally. She shared her plants, ideas, and gardening magazines. Once a gardening friend, always a friend. They don't notice if there is dust in the house, clothes in the basket, or dishes in the sink. They just want to see blooms, buds, and nice flower beds.

It is such a great feeling to give plants to other gardeners. I could hardly wait for Daddy to come up from Carolina to see what was blooming in my garden. We would walk out to the garden first thing, before going in the house. He gave me expert gardening advice, ie,"you've got to pull dirt up around the legs of tomato plants." He also taught me how to sow my turnip salad patch. The weeks passed quickly as I looked forward to him coming back to see if it came up o.k. Looking back, I can see how much validation I really got from him. He left me a wonderful keepsake, a worn out hoe with about 3 inches of metal remaining. My goal is to finish wearing it out, as he often said, "Tis much better to wear out than to rust out." Again, this is applicable to having good physical health; keep moving as long as possible. Gardening is the best pill available; no copayment is required. Lazy people miss out on so much in life. I was blessed to be born into a family of hard- working people. Of course, there are some exceptions in all families.

While digging in the soil, one feels so close to God. He sends the rain and sunshine at just the right time. Like relationships, gardens must be nurtured and appreciated. There is so much to learn from gardening that can be applied in our daily lives. Share observations that paint a good spiritual lesson. When removing a honeysuckle vine from around a prized plant, remind yourself of how sin can wrap around us. The vine becomes mightier than the plant. This is a good children's church demonstration story. Observe how plants thrive from positive attention. Like us, they bend toward the sun for survival. My greatest pleasure is to go out to the garden discovering new plants that pop up in perfect places. My friend Fly and I call them God's little prizes. I love collecting seeds then watching them grow into beautiful plants. Lessons in patience are best learned in a garden. As the seasons pass, keeping a garden journal is a great way of keeping up with the what, when, and where of a growing garden.

Gardening has brought me much joy, happiness, and wholesome living. If there is only two feet of soil available, plant something in the space. Share special tips and some of your gardening secrets with other gardeners. Don't waste time reinventing the wheel. If a special technique worked well for you, tell someone. I've gotten much pleasure from sharing tricks of the trade and formed new friendships in the process. My garden porch parties provide an opportunity to set back and enjoy the fruits of my labor with my gardening friends.   Love the earth and reap rewards abundantly. Your bucket will surely run over.

Hickory Chickens

April, 1996

I really pride myself for knowing more about life in the country than the average person. Ed and I were working on building our house in Java, Virginia. We were only in Java on week-ends, as we were both in the process of retiring from our jobs in North Carolina. We were already acquainted with our closest neighbors, John and Mary Gregory. During this two- year adventure, several people from the community stopped by, asking permission to hunt for hickory chickens on the farm. My curiosity began to rise, as I had no idea what they were talking about. I never heard hickory chickens mentioned in my years on a farm. I just knew about two legged chickens that walked around on the yard. When someone says they ate a chicken off the yard, they meant one of the chickens they raised.

I questioned Eric, a young man from the community. He described them as being shaped like a small tree, cream colored in the mushroom family. He placed them in the category of "good eatins." He mentioned that they grow in damp places, under shade trees near a creek, especially under poplar trees. There are a lot of poplar trees and a nice winding creek on the farm. Ed gave him permission and off to the woods he hurried with his empty loaf bread bag in hopes of finding his supper meal. I looked forward to his return with this special delicacy, as I wanted to know how he planned to prepare them for eating. He must have been gone for about two hours. He returned with a nice packed bag of hickory chickens. I looked at one which was indeed a mushroom, but now I could call them mushrooms. According to him, they required gently washing, drying off, cutting in half lengthwise, dipping in flour and fried in oil, avoiding over-cooking. Since then, I have not asked for hickory chickens in a restaurant, but I have requested mushrooms. This is a great pastime, a chance to be in the woods, enjoying the land and all that we take for granted these days, the trees, the creek, and those little mushrooms hiding under the leaves of poplar trees. To search for them before late March and after April is not recommended. They are definitely a spring welcoming sign.

After learning all about hickory chickens, a great friend, Judy Wagoner came for a visit to see how the house was coming along. We decided to go look for these treasures. We headed for the creek, expecting to find at least one. We searched diligently, scratching under leaves and bark under poplar trees. Not one could we find, but we did see some fools' gold in the creek. It was so fine, sliding right through our hands. The sunlight felt good peeping through the tall trees. We hated to go back to the crowd without hickory chickens. When we returned, a black gentleman from the neighborhood, Mr. George Glass, was talking to the men, getting ready to hunt for hickory chickens. He was well experienced as he had hunted them for years every spring on our farm. Mr. Glass was only gone for thirty minutes, returning with a stuffed bag of chickens. He so much enjoyed telling Judy and me how easy they were to find. He is no longer with us. I will not forget the pleasure on his face and the good conversation that followed his experience that spring day.

Sprinkled With Humor

This reinforces my belief that we are all ignorant, only on different subjects. For those who are reading this, please only look for hickory chickens in the months of March and April. Also, if you are not sure of what a poplar tree looks like, please ask someone. There is so much to be learned from the woods and nature. Too, our neighbors have much to share when we show interest in their stories and experiences. My retirement to do list is getting longer and longer. I wish you the best of luck on your next venture in the woods in the spring time.

Hog Killing Day

(Any day that Daddy thought was right)

Hog killing day for us happened every year. After all, hogs can't be fed forever; they must be eaten sooner or later. There was always some carrying on about this special day. Some in the family felt they had more pressing things to do; maybe it was a bad time to miss school, or maybe it was just too cold. Two or three of us would have to miss school, and it didn't matter if exams were scheduled, if we had dates that night, or if it was too cold. Daddy would even pick Christmas Eve if the weather was right.

Daddy raised our hogs on the farm. He always believed in the principle that two pigs would eat better than one. I guess it could be compared to monkeys doing better with a good partner. Much preparation went into this event, perhaps, two or three days in advance. Salt was purchased, the smokehouse cleared and cleaned, the wash pot set up, knives sharpened, the hog scalder put down, and several good strong men contacted who didn't mind work as we know it. Daddy didn't have too much use for a man standing around with his hands in his pockets all dressed up, especially at a hog killing. Of course, there would always be one or two onlookers waiting for the whiskey to be passed at the end of the day.

My oldest brother "Sambo" was usually chosen to do the shooting, as he is an expert marksman, able to hit the hog exactly above the center of the eyes. Too, he was on time and never one to delay matters. To this day, he is still an on- time man, ready to meet any challenge put before him. The women would prepare pans, pots, etc. and ready themselves to cut up the meat. There were certain pots for certain sections of the meat, one for the sausage, one for fat for lard making, one for ribs and backbone, one for the liver and brains, and one for the whatever, as there is usually one person helping outside the family, that does not know how to separate the meat. Not meaning to omit this important part of the hog, are the guts or chitterlings. Yes, somebody always wanted them and the pig feet too. There was very little wasted. I still have a large "pig foot jar" that came from an old country store.

The lard was about ready to "pour up" around 3 p.m. in the afternoon. The clear hot liquid grease was poured through a strainer, that held the cracklins. Today cracklins are comparable to dried meat skins. We did not own a sausage grinder, as there was at least 200 lbs. of meat to grind. It was taken to town; however, in later years when we killed one hog, we borrowed a grinder from our cousin, Monk Whitt. Like anything mechanical, it would malfunction, causing everything to come to a sudden halt. My sister, Jo Ann was the one who knew more about getting it back to running after some harsh words were spoken to that sausage grinder. The first cake of sausage was sampled for supper and tenderloin fried. Because Daddy was the first to kill hogs, several pounds of meat left the kitchen with the relatives who came to help. This always caused Ma ma a lot of grief. You know, we will always have our takers and givers. After supper, the sausage had to be "worked up", meaning mixing the seasoning well with the meat. Daddy was always good at seasoning sausage just right. Ma ma would not let him season it hot. To get an aged taste, the sausage was put into cloth bags. The remainder was bagged for freezing.

The next day was spent cleaning up the kitchen, washing all the big pots, and getting borrowed things back to the lenders. The reputation for good sausage caused people to start calling Daddy for a few pounds. He had no problem getting $2.25 a pound. He kept a list of names with the details. He was also known to cut the heart out of a ham, the section having the most lean meat, for a cousin who lived miles away dropping by for a visit. Sharing part of a country ham was about the only thing he had to share. Years ago it was common for hams to be given to a doctor in lieu of money for a debt owed. Farmers worried if they could not pay their debts, big or small.

Now, there are some other things about hog killings that the younger family members liked, especially hearing adult conversations about the family dynamics, the latest news about how hard times were and how they were going to make it through the winter all sprinkled with country humor. There was much said about "making do." If my generation of today knew about "making do," there would be enough savings set aside for them to be able to comfortably retire at age 50. Perhaps, the days of raising hogs on the farm and hog killings will return some day. Until then, I will enjoy my bacon and ham as often as possible. Of course, what we buy now is just not the same, but thinking about the old days of hog killings makes for a good breakfast meal. Once in a restaurant, I asked a waitress if she had country ham, and she replied, "Honey have you ever seen a pig raised in the city?" I liked her humor which was very appropriate for my comment. There are plenty of hog killings going on in the Mountainous areas of the country. I just might take a ride up into the hills to see this event once again. They might even let me help bag up the sausage.

Sprinkled With Humor

I almost forgot something. Country folk know how to do something the easiest way. I once saw chitterlings, which are the guts of the hog, being washed in an old wringer type washing machine. This was a pretty clever idea. Maybe the machine was used solely for that purpose at that particular house. Perhaps a new automatic washing machine had replaced the old wringer washer. Does it really matter?

Below are pictures of my family participating in a hog killing in the late eighties.

Ready to be cut open

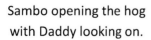

Sambo opening the hog with Daddy looking on.

Ed Little and Sambo
Adcock cutting out the
backbone.

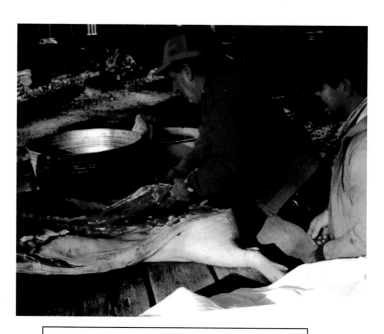

Removing the spareribs, will carve out
one of the hams next.

Cousin Monk Whitt helping out.

Jo Ann Adcock with sister Faye looking on

Daddy and his close friend Sam Tingen

The task of separating the organs that came out of the hog was a challenge. One had to know what to look for. There were always persons in the community who had spoken for the liver, the brains, the feet, and the chitterlings. Actually, there is very little waste after the job is completed. Any pieces of meat that were dropped on the ground were readily eaten up by the yard dogs.

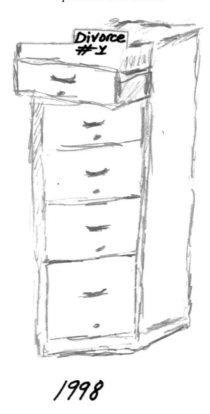

1998

Humor In The File Cabinet

Second marriages bring many challenges. For example, the simple task of merging all files of personal papers, important documents, receipts, etc. for many years. I knew it would be a major undertaking, as I had recognized one of my husband's habits, hoarding. He liked to keep things much longer than I do.

At his request, I started this task. Finding the receipt for his first bicycle was a good sign that there was much more to

43

handle. I cannot say that he did not have a system, as everything was all there and labeled. There were two full file cabinets. Naturally, I became more interested in folders with pictures. There was one that caught my attention. I had heard him tell stories of doing big cookings for various community events in his former home town of Morganton, North Carolina. A new sheriff was to be elected and the race had started with Ed cooking his famous barbecue on his barbecue rig. This particular photo was taken in front of his cooker loaded with barbecue. A woman in tight jeans and a striped top hat was bending over while Mr. Little applied a campaign sticker of his choice for Sheriff on her butt. They all looked to be having a great time. I can only imagine the jokes, laughter, good food, and the politicking going on under that tent. I really wanted more information, but in this case, I will accept that a picture is worth a thousand words.

I continued on searching through papers reflecting hard work, perseverance, dedication to family, loyalty to his friends and a lot of heartache. In the top drawer, I saw a folder with a tab labeled Divorce # 1. Of course I pulled it immediately thinking I might learn something new or maybe something he had failed to tell me. This was not the case. However, being the curious analyst that I am, I found myself laughing at what he must have been feeling at the time he labeled that folder. Perhaps he anticipated a number two or three divorce down the road. I decided to show him this folder when he came home for dinner. I should have known that he would not see the humor in this.

When he arrived, the folder was in plain view on the kitchen table. I started laughing and he did not see anything funny whatsoever. He is a pretty serious guy most of the time. I shared some words of encouragement about our marriage and voiced the likelihood of no other divorces occurring. We are now in our 29th year and it has not been mentioned since. As often said, men cannot read our minds, nor can they know our feelings if we keep them inside. I never thought that this file cabinet would bring

Sprinkled With Humor

such a nice memory to add to my funny files. He gave me permission to share it in my presentations. You can expect to find humor most any place. There are endless ways of communicating our thoughts, feelings, fears, and humor with families and friends. It is up to us to figure out the best way of doing so; that helps everyone in the end.

Humor In The Workplace

(1968-1997)

As a Nursing educator, I was often required to give presentations on health and wellness issues, infection control practices and other health- related matters. Training sessions were done in small groups or large audiences.

My job required meeting with professional staff as well as persons who might not have a high school education. My previous experiences as a nurse prepared me for the challenge. I had twenty years working directly with mentally ill patients and knew anxiety when I saw it.

The hospital auditorium was used for training when large numbers were in attendance. Much of the information was boring but required of every employee. I could always tell who was having a hard time listening, see the uncomfortable employees who felt out of place, and those who came because they had to come. With my appreciation for the benefits of humor, I designed a cartoon that proved to be perfect for everyone. About ten minutes prior to the presentations, I used the following on a slide. The laughter would start, getting all relaxed and ready to listen. Yes, a picture is worth a thousand words. Over the years, I have collected several signs, cartoons, and wall plaques that are great for ice breakers. We run into people from all walks of life who cannot see the humor around them. Share your sense of humor with them and pass the story on. Consider yourself lucky if your Doctor has a good sense of humor.

Listen To Your Children

(1975-until)

Parenting can consume us to the point that we stop listening to what our children have to say. We get busy with life: making a living, meeting deadlines, and fighting the crowd. We forget children really do have something to say. Because of my divorce I became a single parent, so having time for listening was even less available. I soon learned that I needed to start listening closely.

My dear son, Jason called me one day, saying "Maaa, I know now why they call it take home pay. It's because you don't have enough left to do anything else but go home."

My son, performing work outside a major eating establishment, Bojangles in Danville, Virginia, shared with me that hungry people will hurt you. He was trying to finish up some shrubbery trimming, needing only one more minute. A lady begin yelling at him, as he was keeping her from getting her chicken box. She took off and barely missed hitting him. He advised me, "Don't agitate a hungry people, they will hurt you." His observation is true, I think most people are easier to get along with and more likeable when not in a state of hunger.

Jason never ate as much as I thought he should. Frequently,

Sprinkled With Humor

I would gently nag him to eat more of this or that. After becoming an adult, he had a different explanation. He said, "Mama, people are killing themselves every day with forks and spoons." Being a nurse and well aware of obesity and its consequences, I never looked at this problem through his lens. I don't ask him to eat more now. He falls into the category of eating to live versus living to eat. There is a huge difference.

I enjoy hearing adults sharing what their grandchildren have told them. A distant cousin shared that as she was spanking her six year old grandson, he told her, "Grandma, you could have a heart attack while hitting me." The laughing started and she never completed the task. It's enlightening to know that children know how to use humor to distract from the present. Pay more attention to the little tots and what they have to say. They know when people don't listen to them. When they become adults, they still know when they are being ignored.

Nuggets, Sayings, and Advice Picked Up Along The Way

If I did not hear it at school, I heard it by eavesdropping from my relatives, neighborhood gatherings, and the community grapevine, which is known for passing on unverified facts. Some of what I heard has been helpful to me in my adult life. I am still listening just in case something new might be of value in my later years. I have shaken my memory to recall who said what and stated their names when able. I've also listed captions from some of my favorite signs and billboards. For the benefit of my relatives, I included some of their advice as well as my own. I have referenced many of them during my presentations to various audiences. I have observed some in the audience writing them down. The value of listening to others is reinforced in my mind. If you haven't heard it, then it can't be passed on.

"Nothing is more expensive than ignorance." -Ruth Askins, Nursing Instructor

"Try to do something every day for someone who cannot return the favor." -Daddy

"The best way to raise a child is by living a good example" -Mary Davis, Sunday School Teacher, Trinity United Methodist Church, my home church.

"When you go by the dump, throw out your bad attitude, your grudges, and your prejudices along with the trash. It will make you a better employee, a better neighbor, and a better parent."

-Staff Development Instructor, John Umstead Hospital, Butner North Carolina

"Try to leave things better than you found them." -Daddy

"Two pigs eat better than one." -Daddy (I think he was implying you were better off married.)

"Son, don't bring home anything that eats." -Faye Little's advice to her teenage son)

"Honey child, don't let your rear end run away with your brains tonight." -Aunt Cora

"New Members Needed, Perfect People Need Not Apply."

- Church Marquee near Burlington, N.C. -Author unknown

"Do you know what I got for my Birthday……..five baby kittens, Lula, Louise, Lois, Lisa, and Lana." -Faye Little's Response to telemarketers

"While in life's waiting room, take the opportunity to use humor in your interactions." - Faye Little

"All our customers make us happy, some when they come, some when they leave." -Sign in bathroom of old Leggett Department store, Roxboro, N.C. -Author unknown

"Try to be a rainbow in somebody's cloud." -Maya Angelou

"Be kind to your children; they will choose your nursing home." -Hallmark card adapted

"Yes, this is my truck. No, I will not help you move." -Sign on truck in Danville, VA. Female driver unknown

"I started out with nothing and still have something left." -Sign on truck in Chatham County, North Carolina. -Owner unknown

"Go home and love your family." -Mother Teresa

Sprinkled With Humor

"Working for the Lord doesn't pay much, but the rewards are out of this world." -Written on a tee shirt worn by a woman at the Altavista flea market in Virginia.

"Lord, I have a very busy schedule today, things to do, places to go, people to meet; in case I forget you, don't you forget me."

-Sign on wall in Mrs. Wilborn's Restaurant outside South Boston, VA. -Author unknown

"Sometimes I drive my truck and sometimes I go with my Brother-in-law." -Response by John Gregory when asked for directions to Altavista

"Son, marry an ugly woman; she will stay the same and won't turn on you." -Uncle Jonah.

"Girls, don't wear shoes that hurt your feet; the pain will show on your face." -Mrs. Boyd, Home Economics teacher, Webb High School, Oxford, N.C.

"I've read so much about the bad effects of smoking, drinking, and sex that I have decided to give up reading." -sign on kitchen wall at Uncle Ben's house

"You are better off living alone than with the wrong person."

-Aunt Janie Ruth

"Put only good things on your Bucket List." -Faye Little

"Be ready in case the bus comes." -Faye Little

"Maaaa, more folks are killing themselves with forks and spoons than from smoking." -Jason Huff

"It is better to have it and not need it than to need it and not have it." -Sister, Jo Ann

"Don't pity the blind man; instead, pity the man who has good eyesight and still can't see." -Reverend Don Davidson, former pastor Mount Hermon Baptist Church, Danville, Virginia

"That squirrel was so tough that I could not stick a fork in the gravy." -Uncle Henry

"It was so windy at my house that it took me and Dolly both to hold a quilt over the key hole." -Uncle Ben

"The one that cries the loudest is not always the one who is hurting the most." -Aunt Corrina

"I can't control the wind, but I can adjust my sail." -Jimmy Dean

Maaa Leaves Home

(Fall of 1997)

For years, I've listened to Moms tell their versions of what it was like to have their sons and daughters leave home. I recall quite well leaving home to marry at age 18. To leave home at age 48 was a bit different.

I knew for the last eight years that I would move from my birth place in Granville County to live in Java, Virginia. Visiting the farm in Virginia gave me many opportunities to learn what the area was like. Planting a flower garden and tomatoes reassured me that the same opportunities I had in Berea were also in Virginia. Ed and I decided that moving was the best option, as we were both in second marriages. His life time dream was to be able to live on his farm in Virginia. We started building a house on the farm in the winter of 1995. Trips to Virginia were made on week-ends. Ed had many friends whom he had helped on their building projects over the years. Many of them returned the favor, helping on our house. My job was to prepare them lunch at least twice. I would return to Berea with pots of leftover food, dirty clothes, and a long list of what we needed to take back the next week end. The closest thing to entertainment was going to the dump on Sunday afternoon. After two years, the house was finished and moving day was approaching.

I began having serious talks with Jason about the responsibilities of running a home. At the time, he did not want to move with us. During these discussions, the need for him to go back to school always surfaced. He had gotten accustomed to making some money and chose to delay any educational goals. We talked about potatoes a lot and how many ways they could be used to avoid going to bed hungry. He grabbed one and laughed about my vivid financial details. I promised to leave him a bag of potatoes, some bath soap, and laundry detergent.

Ed and I decided to make our move official on Labor Day week-end. The number of loads we had to move was greatly reduced by the fact of us moving things gradually for eight years. Packing accumulated stuff for 21 years brought several things to mind. Memories of how it all started, the changes that occurred, and what still needed to be done. Decisions had to be made about what to do with old things, family pictures, pots with no handles, etc. Of course, not having a deadline made things much easier. Movers can learn a lot about themselves by making inventories of what they hold on to, things they would not let go of or refused to throw away. Apparently I have a fetish for dishes, especially cake plates. I've asked a close friend to not allow me to bring home any more dishes of any kind on our shopping trips. Even now, this does not always work. I always end up in the kitchen area of estate sales, and so does my friend, Emily. I got Jason to stand in the kitchen to help me decide about what I should take or leave. He was not especially glad to do this, as it was becoming more real that he would be planning meals, buying groceries, keeping the house straight, and being responsible for the entire household.

I kept telling myself, "I have to let go and let him meet this challenge." I knew he was very capable. As we drove away,

Sprinkled With Humor

Jason was repairing the mailbox door. He said, "Maaa, when are you coming back?" When beyond the curve, the tears came as I looked in the rearview mirror reflection of the last 48 years of living within a mile of my birthplace. Adapting and moving on is a part of life. I had new goals and plans for our new home in Virginia. I look forward to Jason telling me his version of "Maaa leaves home."

After 20 years, we feel settled in and a part of the community. Jason met a gal from Danville, Virginia, Mitzi Denny Powell. They married on our front porch in 2008. They now live in their new home on our farm. We still share lessons on life, have long mom to son talks, and laugh about the family dynamics back home. I go back to Berea at least once a month and attend funerals of my kin and friends I left behind. Virginia is now home to me and I am glad I got here as quick as I did.

Moving To Java, Virginia
(Fall of 1997)

Moving day from my neighborhood, my family, my church family, and my lifetime friends finally came. The move only involved a distance of 65 miles, to a rural area in Java, Virginia. The frequent visits here to my husband's family farm made me very familiar with my new home. But, I soon learned that my accent would sound funny to my neighbors, country slogans and sayings would be different, and the make-up of the neighborhood was very different. Even the obituaries read differently. In Virginia, the obits stated where they thought the person ended up........she has gone to her heavenly home, she is now with her family at last, or she joined her master today. Back home, these kind of statements were omitted from the obits. I guess folks just sat around on the tailgates of their pickup trucks and talked about the deceased , drawing their own conclusions.

I soon learned how much more conservatively Virginians lived. They even saved wear and tear on the gate hinges by crawling under the gate. Women described a good man as one who would let the wife keep any change found in the washing machine. Turning the shirt collars was a way of wearing the shirt a little longer. Boiled potato peelings were used as dog food for the stray dogs, of which there was no shortage. Hanging clothes on the line was the norm. The clothes lines in Java were designed with many factors in mind. I immediately approved of them, as they kept roaming animals from chewing the clothes, rain from beating dirt on the clothes, and provided the convenience of reeling them down while standing on the house porch. Two pulley wheels threaded with smooth wire, with one end attached high up on a pole or tree, and the other anchored on the porch, made the perfect clothes line. I really wanted one at my house, but it never got off the, "when I get around to it," list. This is all good as we can all learn a thing or two about being more conservative.

We had great neighbors, the Gregorys, whose family homesite was well established. There are three generations living in the area with jobs close by. My first friendships started at Gregory's Saw Mill with Mary Gregory and Emily Ragsdale.

My first good laugh started with John, the owner of the saw mill. I knew we would laugh about things, as a sign in his office read, "Saddle your horse before cussing out the boss." I was really interested in finding a flea market in the area. After asking around, I learned of one in the town of Altavista, Virginia. I decided that the best person to get directions from would be John. I found him sitting on his front porch one Sunday evening in his favorite attire, Carhartt bib overalls. He is a hard worker and one not to sit on the porch very often. He is an avid fan of The Andy Griffith Show. "John, how do you get to Altavista from here?" His response, "Well sometimes I drive my truck, and sometimes I go with my brother-in-law." It was then I realized I would fit right in and that my communication skills were very adequate.

People mind their own business in Java. We had a small woods fire on the farm, amounting to what my husband would call a "prescribed burn". The next morning, he was approached by a local store owner/neighbor, asking, "I saw a lot of smoke your way yesterday; were you cooking a pig?" The men in the area, liked to keep Farm Tags on their wife's vehicle, meaning she really should stay within five miles of home. They were accustomed to having lunch prepared at home, with the wife being very available at all times. Of course, there was really no place to go except to visit a neighbor or to church. Needless to say, this custom was not used at our house.

The people were quite resourceful in many ways. If a family member or neighbor had an accident, getting them back to the house was easy. They might use a tractor with a big dump bucket on the front to move the injured from the accident site to the ambulance. It was much quicker and safer and the injured person got to tell their story at the community store and at church. Men were known to give their wives a cemetery plot for their birthdays. Of course, if she didn't use it that year, it was regifted for the next year, a great investment for the money.

My first assignment came from Ed. He needed to replace the leather belt to the hand crank of his 1926 T. Model. He gave me the torn leather piece to take with me to the leather shop in Chatham, Virginia. I expected to find a shop full of old men sitting around, chewing the fat about the weather, women, and other unmentionable subjects. Sure enough, when I entered, there they were, sitting around the stove. In the meantime, I waited for several minutes to be greeted. A small dog came up to me, jumped on my foot, and started an exercise in futility. Being somewhat embarrassed, I changed my stance, trying to get him off my foot. He jumped on the other foot and started to climb my leg. Those men sat there, enjoying themselves with entertainment they obviously liked. Finally, I had to forget I was a lady, slinging my leg to get the little darling off. Still the owner, had not come to help me. As I stood there, I looked around the shop, seeing a sign posted clearly in view. It was of help in understanding where I was, as the sign read……..

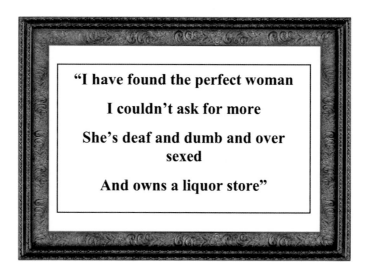

"I have found the perfect woman
I couldn't ask for more
She's deaf and dumb and over sexed
And owns a liquor store"

The men saw me reading the sign. I knew the owner was bound to walk up to help me sooner or later. That was the longest wait I have ever endured, but I learned that the men in this part of the country were cut from the same mold as in Carolina. I got the replacement belt and hurried back home to share my morning experience. The shop no longer exists and most of those men are probably having precious memories, laughing about the little dog and that woman who could not get him off her foot. I hope the dog is doing well and is over his "hormonal surge."

We have lived here since 1997; we know we made a great choice. Many of my fears were proven to be wrong, making me glad the move is a part of my journey. I found a place to share my turnip salad patch and a big front porch for my friends who visit. More wonderful neighbors have settled here adding to the community hub. Perhaps, someday we can have our own Java flea market with lots of little dogs running around.

Ordinary People With Great Humor

I am so grateful for inheriting the skill of talking to strangers. It has enhanced my understanding of many socioeconomic backgrounds, situations, and humanity in general. I am always looking and listening for a good story sprinkled with humor. At times, they would only be one liners. Some are too good not to pass on.

In a local Walmart, I took a seat beside this forlorn looking man. Quickly, we started a conversation. His spill lasted a few minutes. He said, "I brought my wife in here for a loaf of bread and some toilet paper. She has been here for the last two hours. I am seriously thinking of ordering a pizza, as supper is about three hours away. Have you seen her?" I did not know his wife nor him personally. I started to laugh, offering ideas on what she might be doing. I shared that women include many things in their shopping trips, ie, seeing church people, old neighbors, and looking for coupons to use on items they don't need. He calmed down a bit as if he had learned something new about women. I enjoyed our laughing and gained some insight on men and what makes them irritable when with their wives shopping. I bet she didn't have a driver's license and depended on him to take her. Maybe I will meet her the next time, as I already have plenty of suggestions.

The Night Shift Supervisor was pregnant with baby number seven. Of course, curious people wanted to know why she wanted so many children. Her response was one that I had never heard of, despite hearing strange reasons why multiple pregnancies occur. She was quite serious in her reply. "Well, it's very simple; my husband and I live very close to a railroad track. The train comes through every morning about 4 a.m. It is too early to get up, and too late to go back to sleep." Since this was so original, I wrote it down to share with other ladies who might have to answer such a question.

Being raised in a poverty area, I wanted to know if other people lived like we did. Seeing the movie," Gone With The Wind" was a real treat for most of the school children. Our history teacher deemed it necessary. If the school did not recommend a specific movie, many moons passed before kids in the country saw a movie. We entertained ourselves by making play houses in the woods, using any discarded items we could find. My love for decorating most likely started from this childhood activity. The boys were more resourceful. They invited city boys to come go fishing in local ponds. The motive being to gain access to real fishing lures and nicely stocked tackle boxes. Preparation would start a couple of days in advance of the expected visit. They would roam the neighborhood, looking for some worn out bed springs. After finding one, they would lower the springs into a special place in the pond. When the fishing escapade started, the visitors wanted to know where the best spot was to hang the big one. Of course, they were always told to throw in the direction of the sunken bed springs. The nice lures and fishing tackle would be firmly attached to the bed springs, making the visitors think the big fish broke the line. These country boys knew how to get what they wanted, in a devious way. Some of the visitors became successful businessmen, and the home boys are still fishing, using the same fishing tackle.

Misunderstandings and More

In the summer of 2015, traveling to Pigeon Forge, Tennessee, gave me an opportunity to talk to people of other regions. Stopping at a country store gave me a chance to share my accent with a stranger. I did not know that I was going to have fun doing so. I was so impressed with the cleanliness of this particular store. It was immaculate, especially the bathroom. I decided to tell the owner how much I appreciated his clean place. I initiated the conversation, which lasted maybe five minutes. He wanted to know where we were headed and directed one question to me. "How far do you live from Ward Burton?" I immediately started laughing, as I very well knew he was referring to my country accent. I replied, "about twenty-five miles." He laughed, saying "I knew you came from somewhere in his neck of the woods." We laughed together and I've had fun passing this on. It would be a boring world if we all talked the same.

Hearing loss can cause multiple communication problems, ie, hearing what was not intended, not hearing what was meant, and filling in the gaps with what you thought was said. My phone rung at 9:30 p.m. one night, somewhat close to retiring for the day. It was a long- time friend of mine, who was doing some ancestry research in Virginia. "Faye, I am in the area and wanted to come by your house; would like you to meet my beau." I shared this with my other half, who is very hard of hearing. He replied, "We are not going to Bojangles this late!" I had a hard time trying to restrain myself. I explained to him that she was interested in me meeting her boyfriend. He only heard the word Bo, and filled in the gaps to complete what he thought I said.

Daddy loved to ride most any place, especially after he became less confident in his driving. We often just rambled over country roads, old places, cemeteries and into small towns. He was a great passenger, never criticized my driving or complained of the trips. The conversations we had are priceless now. He had been wearing a hearing aid for three years or more, still getting adjusted to noises and other annoyances that come with hearing aid devices. As we were riding down the road, a loud beeping sound occurred very consistently. He started to complain how badly he hated the hearing aid, threatening to throw it out the window if it didn't stop. I knew it was the seat belt and not the hearing aid. Of course, it stopped after fastening his seat belt. We continued on with our trip, laughing about this among other things. We could always find something to laugh about in the past or present.

I had been invited to speak at a nice Nursing Home in North Carolina. The meeting was held in a large dining room. The patient population contained many residents in wheelchairs. I arrived early and got settled in the spot reserved for me. There were two ladies who wanted to sit at the table directly in front of me in their wheelchairs. After speaking for about ten minutes, I noticed they were both getting very restless, talking back and forth to each other. I did not get too alarmed, after all, they were at home. The lady who invited me, came over to speak to them, asking them to refrain from talking while I was talking. After my session ended, the facilitator approached me, with uncontrolled laughter. She wanted to tell me why those ladies got so perturbed.

One lady told the other one, "I want to go back to my room, she has been talking ten minutes and she ain't sung yet." Most every occasion involved someone singing to them, so they expected the same kind of entertainment from me that day. After this, I decided to do my introductions a bit differently. We can never rehearse enough to stop human beings from being themselves as these ladies were. It just made my day much more memorable.

Waiting rooms of doctors' offices, can be interesting. People enjoy talking about their ailments as long as they have an audience. Too, it beats sitting there in silence. Although, much is preached about privacy, actually there is much to be desired. Our names are still called when we are ready to be seen. I guess this is better still than having a number for a name. While waiting to be seen, I heard two ladies talking next to me. One lady asked the other, "Why are you being seen today?" She replied, "I am having trouble with my blood pressure medication, and why are you here today?" She said, "The last time I was here, my doctor told me if I didn't lose weight, the next test he did on me would be an autopsy, so I reckon he will do that today." The lady seemed rather serious, and I did not correct her, but it would have been interesting to see if she told her doctor what test she was expecting to have.

I was a student nurse, eager to solve all problems for all people. Patient teaching was a great opportunity to share new information, clarify misunderstandings, and to share resources. I was assigned to a patient who was in the hospital for the third time with pancreatitis. Her chart indicated alcohol was indeed the cause. My instructor was adamant that I emphasize cause and effect with her on this issue. She was a nice lady, very engaging, and cooperative. We talked about her history, her admissions, and what happened in between. She shared that she had not maintained sobriety for more than a few weeks after discharge. I asked her if she had ever been told about AA. Her response was, "I switched to Ancient Age and it made me just as drunk as the other liquor." Someone assumed she knew what AA was. We talked about the Alcoholics Anonymous program for quite a while. She seemed relieved to know that there actually might be hope for her. In closing, I felt good about our session. Perhaps, she got involved in AA and is sober today. This was a strong reminder to me as a nurse how we assume our patients know about resources available, have an understanding of what is happening to them, and know of preventive health measures. I will always remain a strong advocate of patient teaching in any setting. It is much easier to change what we acknowledge.

A similar scenario occurred in a doctor's office while a student nurse. My job was to help get the patient prepared for the exam. A frail man came in, giving a brief history of his recent heart attack. As he undressed for the exam, I noticed his small thin body was almost covered in Nitro patches. He told me, "I am really here today because I cannot find another place to put a patch." Again, someone in the medical profession failed to tell him to take off the old patch before applying a new one. I shall not forget the image standing before me so innocently. Perhaps we are in too big of a hurry not paying attention to the patient's level of education. It is our responsibility to pass on information to our patients. I fear that technology is replacing patient education on all levels. I am sure there are people walking around covered with old patches and hearing aids with no batteries. In the words of a former Nursing Instructor, "Nothing is more expensive than ignorance." I have this to be so true in my own life experiences.

Explanations and Colloquialisms

For readers who might question what I meant by certain phrases, sayings, and references, I have explained them in my own words.

White Lightning (Lightnin)................... (Non- tax- paid whiskey with high alcohol content, made in a remote area not under the jurisdiction of the government. The song, " White Lightning" was recorded by an American Music Artist, George Jones in 1959, becoming a #1 hit for him.

Sibship................... Brothers and sisters having the same parents

Hard times................... Trying to make ends meet by whatever means/resources available

Going into town................... Leaving home to go to a nearby city, often about 15 miles away by car only when necessary.

Pig foot jar................... A tall, barrel- shaped jar with a lid, often used in country stores to display pickled pig feet. Customers would purchase one or two pig feet at a time, eating them in the store.

Chewing the fat................... A small group of men or women sitting around on stools or benches at country stores, talking about the last time it rained, how bad the corn looked, and what was going on among the neighbors. Most any subject might come up for discussion.

Lard .... The end product from cooking the fat portions cut from the hog at hog-killing time , cooked outside in a large black iron pot. Mostly used for baking biscuits and for recipes requiring lard, which is equivalent to Crisco.

Hand- me- down pile................... A collection of clothes worn by older family members who no longer wore them, handing them down to the younger children. These were worn out before new clothes were bought.

Cash money crops................... Often included garden produce raised on the farm, tobacco grown as a sole means of making a living, and grains produced on a farm that were sold for cash money.

Out buildings................... Structures located fairly close to the living quarters for convenience: could be the wood house, barns, smokehouse for storing meat, the outhouse that served as toilets, and tool sheds designated for certain items.

Fools' gold .... Shiny small rock fragments often seen in clear water in a creek. The sun light shining on them makes them appear as gold.

Home Economics Class .... Included in High School curriculums 50 years ago as a requirement for girls, providing an opportunity for learning the basics of sewing, preparing meals, housekeeping, and correct etiquette.

Community grapevine .... A means of passing on information to neighbors, friends, and others in a community. After much repetition, the validity could be questioned. This concept of communication is still common today. When questioned about the source, one might respond, "I heard it through the grapevine."

Prescribed burn .... A term used in Forestry meaning the fire was intentionally set to a designated area to eradicate debris. This was a supervised activity.

AA .... Alcoholics Anonymous, a voluntary fellowship of men and women that focuses on principles of recovery for alcohol addiction. AA has the reputation of being the best resource available for successful recovery.

Hickory chicken ……………….. A mushroom that can be found growing in the woods, particularly under poplar trees in the spring time. They are usually fried for eating.

Hanging out……………….. A term used by teenagers to describe being on a date: might involve being among others in a shop, restaurant, or some other public place other than at home.

Hog Killing ……………….. An annual event for most families in the country, involving neighbors bartering with each other for manpower necessary for getting the job done successfully, meaning by sundown the hog meat was salted down in the smoke house, the sausage stored in bags, the lard in cans, and all utensils washed and stored for the next year.

Watering hole……………….. A place where men or women gather to indulge in the spirits, which might include beer, whiskey, wine, and other mind-altering substances, doing so without disapproval from their peers. If a woman needed her man for an emergency, she could usually find him at the neighborhood watering hole.

Puttin ……………….. A dessert often made up of wild berries and fruit, or whatever was raised on the farm. Large metal pans were used because of large families. Children enjoyed eating from the pan versus eating from a dessert plate.

Getting something started................... Catching the attention of onlookers, especially teenagers with some new idea in fashion, hoping for a change

Mind your own business................... Something most every child raised in the country was told by their parents. Meddling into other peoples' affairs was frowned upon and labeled as nosy.

Bib overalls.................... Worn by most farmers due to being very comfortable, especially for jobs requiring bending and stooping. They were sold in solid blue or striped denim. Depending upon how the tobacco sold, farmers were very happy if there was enough money left to buy two pair. Women can be seen wearing them now, most likely for the same reasons.

Sharing Stories in the Community

SUBMITTED PHOTO

HUMORIST SPEAKS AT AARP MEETING

AARP held its monthly meeting for November in the fellowship hall of First Baptist Church. Guest speaker was Faye Little, registered RN and humorist. President Kay Lewis (left) welcomes Little who presented a program laced with humorous anecdotes of rural life and people in her daily life within Halifax and surrounding counties. AARP meets the third Tuesday of each month all year long. A catered lunch is offered at the end of each meeting. For information on joining, call Kay Lewis at 572-1641.

Presentation to the Young at Heart Club at Rivermont Baptist Church, Danville, Virginia October 16, 2007

Country Cousins Garden Club

The garden club was organized in 2007 . Members share plants, seeds, ideas, tricks of the trade, and visit favorite nurseries. Garden tours and parties are held in the spring time at their homes.

Left to Right: Marie Harris Pridgen, Margaret Ford, Jesse Barksdale, Faye Little and Rochelle Lee

Gardening Results

Java Gardens

Granville County Words of Praise
By: Faye Little

Granville County is a good place to be

There are many opportunities that are free

There are pastures with horses to ride

And slides of tobacco waiting to be tied

You can go camping, swimming, or fishing

If you aren't in Granville county, look what you are missing

Among its' trees, land, and hills

You might find an old cider mill

If you like old houses and mud-dobbed barns

You will probably want to visit one of its' farms

By now, you can tell from these words of praise

Granville County is where I was raised.

ABOUT THE AUTHOR

Faye A. Little was born on July 7, 1949, in Person County, North Carolina, living in the Berea community until she moved to Java, Virginia, in 1997. Being one of eight children of a sharecropper, she experienced life's difficulties in rural America. Proud of her heritage, she has grown to appreciate experiences both on and off the farm. A retired Registered Nurse, she lives in the Java community of Pittsylvania County, Virginia. After thirty years of working in a state mental hospital in Butner, North Carolina, she promised herself that if she ventured back into the field of nursing, she would focus on the wellness aspect of health. That view has led to an interest in humor and its contributions to good health. After researching the benefits of a good sense of humor, she decided to provide presentations for various groups: retirees, clubs, seniors and individuals' special occasions. During these presentations, she shares humorous vignettes of everyday life, especially in country settings. She enjoys talking about signs and posters she has observed in various places. When time allows, she ends her talks with her own Pearls of Wisdom points that reflect on inspirational wisdom that have enriched her life, strongly agreeing with Proverbs 17:20 "A merry heart doeth good like a medicine, but a broken spirit drieth the bones." She enjoys retirement, the strong ties with her family back in Carolina, and Mount Hermon Baptist Church where she is involved in the outreach visitation ministry. After several years of presentations to local groups, she was encouraged by her friends to compose some of her stories, sayings, and humor in book form. She hopes, through this book, that her readers are inspired to exercise their sense of humor, easing the burdens of others along the way.

Made in the USA
Columbia, SC
19 February 2019